The Frog Scientist

The Frog Scientist

Pamela S. Turner

Photographs by Andy Comins

 Houghton Mifflin Books for Children
Houghton Mifflin Harcourt
Boston   New York   2009

For Kelsey —Pamela S. Turner

For Nana —Andy Comins

Houghton Mifflin Books for Children is an imprint of
Houghton Mifflin Harcourt Publishing Company.

www.hmhbooks.com

Book design by YAY! Design
The text of this book is set in Eplica.
Photo credits on page 57.

Library of Congress Cataloging-in-Publication Data
Turner, Pamela S.
The frog scientist / by Pamela S. Turner.
p. cm. — (Scientists in the field)
ISBN: 978-0-618-71716-3
1. Frogs—Effect of pesticides on—Juvenile literature.
2. Atrazine—Physiological effect—Juvenile literature. 3.
Hayes, Tyrone—Juvenile literature. I. Title.

QL668.E2T875 2009
597.8'917279—dc22
2008039770

Printed in China
LEO 10 9 8 7 6 5 4 3 2 1

Contents

SONORAN GREEN TOAD

RED-BANDED RUBBER FROG

WAXY-MONKEY TREE FROG

ROCOCO TOAD

The Frog Squad

The sun is just peeking over golden Wyoming hills as Dr. Tyrone Hayes wakes his team. Jasmin Reyes sleeps wrapped in green mosquito netting. "Jasmin, the giant pickle," Tyrone teases. "Get up!"

Two more rumpled heads pop out of the grass: Tyrone's son, Tyler, and Young Kim-Parker. Field biology is not for those who like to sleep in.

LEFT
Leopard frogs eat many insects, such as mosquitoes. They also eat earthworms, snails, and spiders. Frogs keep the world a lot less buggy.

BELOW
Tyrone at Dugway Pond, near Sinclair, Wyoming.

No one stops for breakfast, either. Daybreak is prime frog-catching time. Young walks over to the Dugway Pond, just a few feet from the campsite. She wades out and sinks a glass sample bottle into the cool water.

Tyrone, Jasmin, and Tyler stalk the edges of the pond with nets. Though they try to be sneaky, with each step juvenile leopard frogs scatter in all directions. The hopping frogs look like little green kernels of popping corn.

Jasmin's net slaps down into brown muck at the pond's edge. It comes up empty.

"Get under them," advises Tyrone, pulling a captured frog out of his net.

Young grabs a net and joins Tyrone, Jasmin, and Tyler on the frog hunt. Everyone counts out loud as they add frogs to the collection bag. "Fifteen . . . sixteen . . . seventeen . . ." Their goal: fifty juvenile frogs.

Clouds of tiny mayflies rise over the pond. The scientific name for this kind of insect, *Ephemeroptera*, means "lasting but a day," and that's about all the time an adult mayfly gets. When mayflies reach adulthood they mate and then die within hours, raining from the sky to become frog food. Many of the mayfly-fattened frogs

Jasmin and Tyler look for juvenile leopard frogs.

2

around this pond will, in turn, become food for the two blue herons winging overhead.

This corner of Wyoming seems untouched by humans. The water, air, and sweet-smelling grass are abuzz with life. You wouldn't know it, but even in a place like this there can be pesticides that can harm wildlife.

A pesticide is a chemical designed to kill a "pest"—either a weed or an insect. Every year farmers spray millions of pounds of pesticides on their crops. As rainwater drains off fields, it carries the pesticides with it. The pesticides end up in ponds, streams, and rivers. Pesticides can also stick to tiny bits of dirt. When the wind blows, pesticide-laced dust is swept into the air. The pesticide may end up hundreds of miles from a farmer's field.

Pesticides are not meant to harm frogs. However, when people put pesticides into the environment, the effects can be very hard to control. Tyrone wants to know how pesticides in the environment affect growing frogs.

The collection bag fills with frogs. "Thirty-three," Tyler calls out.

"Thirty-four," says Young.

"Thirty-five, thirty-six, thirty-seven," says Tyrone. He's an expert frog-napper. The barefoot scientist in Wyoming has caught frogs since he was a barefoot kid in South Carolina.

One frog gets sweet revenge. Tyrone lunges—the frog dives—and Tyrone quickly leaps back, snorting and laughing. "Ugh! I just got a reed up my nose!"

The team slowly circles the pond, splashing and squelching through the mud.

ABOVE LEFT
A leopard frog's spots help it hide from predators. When winter comes, leopard frogs snuggle into the mud at the bottom of lakes and ponds and hibernate until spring.

LEFT
Tyrone captures a juvenile leopard frog.

3

"Forty-eight . . . forty-nine . . ." says Tyrone.

"Fifty!" calls Tyler.

These fifty frogs are part of a scientific experiment. Tyrone wants to know if the pesticide atrazine affects the development of these leopard frogs. Tyrone visited Dugway Pond early this spring. When he tested the water, there was no atrazine in it. At the same time, he collected a few clutches of frog eggs to raise back in his laboratory at the University of California, Berkeley.

After taking some frog eggs out of Dugway Pond, Tyrone put a single drop of atrazine into the pond water. (He was given special permission to put atrazine in as part of this experiment.) The atrazine will break down within a few months. Right now the level of atrazine in Dugway Pond is similar to levels found in many ponds and streams around the United States. Although Tyrone doesn't like putting even a tiny pinch of pesticide into the environment, this little pond is part of an experiment that will help answer some big questions.

Tyrone and his team are capturing juvenile frogs that developed from eggs laid in the pond this spring. But there are adult leopard frogs here, too. Tyrone fishes an adult out of the pond and holds it next to a youngster. The adult leopard frog is a male. Adult males have a special pad on their thumb and forearm that they use to clutch the female while mating. "This guy

GREAT BLUE HERON

LEFT
Leopard frogs are an important food for many birds (including great blue herons), snakes (including broad-banded water snakes), and mammals such as foxes, otters, and raccoons.

FAR LEFT
An adult male leopard frog next to a juvenile.

BROAD-BANDED WATER SNAKE

Young, a student at Berkeley, carefully makes labels for each water sample that record date, time, location, temperature, and elevation.

could be the father of this young one," says Tyrone. He looks the juvenile in the eye and demands: "Who's your daddy?"

Young, Jasmin, and Tyler carefully recount the young frogs. Each frog is put into a container with a liquid that will cause a quick and painless death. It is sad, but these few dozen frogs may help save millions of others.

Pesticides like atrazine can have a scary effect on frogs. In earlier lab experiments Tyrone found that atrazine feminized male leopard frogs. Normally, female frogs make eggs and male frogs make sperm. But many male frogs raised in atrazine-contaminated water were deformed. They grew eggs in their testes instead of sperm.

Tyrone wants to compare male Dugway frogs raised in the wild to male Dugway frogs raised in his laboratory. "Frogs are really sensitive to chemicals in the water," explains Tyrone. "Tadpoles have gills, but adults breathe through their skin, as well as using their lungs. And frog eggs don't have shells. They are completely exposed."

Frogs are in serious trouble all over the world. The numbers of many species are declining. "Atrazine may be part of the problem," says Tyrone.

Fewer frogs? Some people might shrug. Yet the frogs may be telling us something important about the health of our environment.

"Even if you don't care about frogs, you have to wonder how this affects *us*, too," says Tyrone. "What's in our water?"

ABOVE

Tyrone prepares and preserves some of the young frogs. Back in the lab, Tyrone and his students will examine the frogs under a microscope.

ABOVE LEFT, LEFT

Tyler and Jasmin count and sort leopard juvenile frogs. Tyler, Tyrone's son, is a middle school student in El Cerrito, California. Jasmin is one of Tyrone's students at Berkeley.

The Frog Kid

Tyrone didn't worry about chemicals in the water when he was younger. He just liked to wade in it. "My neighborhood was near a swamp full of frogs, snapping turtles, and snakes," recalls Tyrone. "My interest in them started when I was four or five. I tell kids, if there is something you like doing, stick with it!"

The Hayes family lived in Columbia, South Carolina. When Tyrone was born in 1967, the American South was still segregated. Tyrone was born in a "colored" hospital—a hospital where only African Americans were treated. White people went to a better hospital, where care was refused to African American patients.

Tyrone shares *What Is a Frog?* with his son, Tyler, and daughter, Kassina. Tyrone's mother gave him the book when he was a little boy.

Tyrone's parents encouraged Tyrone's interest in science. Tyrone's mom bought him a book about frogs. His dad, a carpet installer, brought *National Geographic* magazines home for Tyrone and his two younger brothers.

Tyrone's first lab was his front porch. He kept his frogs, snakes, and lizards there. "My mom wouldn't let them in the house," explains Tyrone. "I dug a big hole in the backyard for my box turtles."

When it was time for college, Tyrone knew he wanted a career in science. He thought that meant becoming a doctor. "I didn't know you could be a research scientist and study frogs," says Tyrone. He applied for admission to just one school: Harvard University. He'd heard it mentioned on a TV show called *Green Acres* and decided it must be good.

Good grades in high school and high test scores got Tyrone into Harvard. He arrived in Boston, Massachusetts, in the fall of 1985. It was difficult to adapt to a bustling city like Boston after growing up in a small, mostly African American town. Tyrone felt out of place.

When Tyrone discovered that students could volunteer to help Harvard professors with research, he knew he'd found what he wanted to do. However, Tyrone needed a job to help pay for college. The only laboratory job he could find was washing

ABOVE
Tyrone, age eight, on Christmas morning.

RIGHT
Tyrone dressed for his Dreher High School prom.

BELOW
Tyrone during a spring break trip to California.

Tyrone poses in front of the Harvard University Science Center during his freshman year.

test tubes, not doing research. Tyrone felt discouraged. His grades went down and he thought about dropping out of college. "I was lost," admits Tyrone.

Two people saved him. One was his girlfriend, Kathy Kim. "Kathy had confidence in me," says Tyrone. The other was Bruce Waldman, a Harvard professor who studied amphibians. Waldman noticed Tyrone's persistence and enthusiasm. "Waldman told me, 'I don't care about your grades. I know you will be a great scientist someday,'" recalls Tyrone. "He gave me a job doing real research."

In Waldman's lab Tyrone studied how temperature affects the development of wood frogs. He found that when the temperature is higher, wood frogs develop faster but are smaller. Temperature also affects the sex ratio—the number of male wood frogs compared to the number of females. Lower temperatures produce more males.

In 1989 Tyrone graduated from Harvard with honors. He and Kathy married and moved to Berkeley, California, for graduate school.

That very same year a gathering of scientists discovered something very frightening. All around the globe, frogs were dying.

Tyrone and Kathy in 1987.

11

Fragile Frogs

A mphibian scientists are like everybody else. They like to talk about what they do.

At an international conference in 1989, nearly everyone was telling the same story. There seemed to be fewer amphibians (frogs, toads, salamanders, and caecilians). Each scientist thought it was happening just to the animals he or she studied. But when the scientists talked to one another, they realized it was happening everywhere.

Amphibian means "double life." Most amphibians begin their life in a watery world, breathing through fishlike gills. Then they transform into an entirely different creature: an air-breathing animal.

BUMBLEBEE
POISON
DART FROG

MOUNTAIN
YELLOW-LEGGED
FROG

STRAWBERRY
POISON
DART FROG

BLUE POISON
DART FROG

PAMPAS TOAD

13

RED-LEGGED
WALKING
FROG

Concerned scientists surveyed amphibian populations all over the world. They discovered that about a third of amphibians (1,856 out of 5,743 species) are threatened with extinction. Since 1980 at least 122 species have probably become extinct.

Australia had a remarkable species called the gastric brooding frog. The mother frog swallowed her eggs and hatched her babies in her stomach. The little frogs hopped from their mother's mouth into the big wide world. During the 1980s, the Australian gastric brooding frogs disappeared.

Something similar happened in Costa Rica. Golden toads once lived in Costa Rica's cool, wet forests. The males of the two-inch-long species were golden orange, like web-footed tangerines. They gathered by the hundreds during breeding season. The golden toad was last seen in 1989. Like the gastric brooding frog, the golden toad is now considered extinct. No one knows what killed the gastric brooding frogs or the golden toads.

Habitat loss is a big problem for many wild animals, including amphibians. Frogs,

ABOVE
This red-legged walking frog from Africa looks like he's wearing tiger-striped underwear. Walking frogs take steps with their hind legs instead of hopping.

RIGHT
The only golden toads left are museum specimens like this one. The species is believed to be extinct.

GOLDEN TOAD

SONORAN DESERT
TOAD

"He looks like a cow turd," Tyrone says affectionately. Although this Sonoran desert toad now lives in Tyrone's lab, the species lives in very dry parts of the American Southwest. They have disappeared from some areas due to habitat loss and pesticide use.

toads, and salamanders die when wetlands are drained, ponds are filled, or forests are cut down. Sometimes amphibian habitat is fragmented (chopped into smaller pieces) when roads, houses, or shopping centers are built. Imagine a tiny frog trying to hop safely across a freeway or parking lot.

Scientists looked closely at places where amphibians were declining. To their surprise, they found it wasn't always where habitat was being lost or fragmented. Frogs were disappearing from protected areas, or places very far from humans. Costa Rica's golden toad lived in a national park. The gastric brooding frog lived in remote parts of Australia.

Deformed frogs appeared, too. In 1995, middle school students in Minnesota found some frogs near a farm. They were juvenile leopard frogs, just like the ones Tyrone

This leopard frog was caught by a child in Reedsburg, Wisconsin. It has an extra leg growing out of its chin. Other deformed frogs were found in the same place.

BLUE POISON DART FROG

ABOVE Blue poison dart frogs live in South America.

RIGHT White's tree frog is found in Australia.

A deadly fungus that threatens frogs was first discovered in these two species.

16

studies. Many of the Minnesota frogs had missing legs, or shriveled legs, or legs that didn't bend. It was strange and scary. People began finding deformed frogs in many other places, too.

What is happening to the world's amphibians?

The answer isn't simple. Amphibian decline has many causes. Since the 1980s the chytrid (pronounced *KIT-rid*) fungus has spread around the world. The disease is killing amphibians in North America, Central America, South America, and Australia. To make matters worse, global warming seems to cause temperatures that help the fungus spread. Though scientists in New Zealand believe they've discovered a chemical that kills the fungus, finding and treating wild frogs would be very difficult.

Some species of frogs living at high altitudes are threatened by ultraviolet (UV) radiation. Man-made chemicals have thinned the ozone layer in our atmosphere. The earth's ozone layer keeps most of these damaging UV rays from reaching us. At high altitudes the air is thinner, and if thin air is combined with a thin ozone area, even more UV radiation reaches the earth. High levels of UV radiation can kill the delicate, shell-less eggs of amphibians that live in mountain areas.

Amphibians are also threatened by introduced species. An introduced species is a creature that shows up somewhere it isn't normally found. The bullfrog, a kind of frog that *isn't* declining, is native to

WHITE'S TREE FROG

17

AMERICAN BULLFROG

the eastern and midwestern parts of the United States. It has been introduced by humans into ponds and streams all over the West. Introduced bullfrogs gobble up smaller native frogs and take over their habitat. Sometimes fish are introduced into lakes and streams so fishermen will have something to catch. The non-native fish usually have a taste for the native tadpoles.

Often a frog species faces not just one threat but many. California's red-legged frog has been hit by a truckload of problems: habitat loss, fungal disease, and introduced bullfrogs and fish. And if all that weren't enough, red-legged frogs are also killed by pesticides sprayed on crops in California's Central Valley. The pesticides are blown by the wind into the foothills where many of the remaining frogs live.

And those scary frog deformities? Scientists found that some frog deformities are caused by a parasite. The parasite is a worm that burrows under a tadpole's skin and disrupts the tadpole's growth. It may prevent a leg from growing or cause deformed legs.

Bullfrogs are very aggressive and prey on other frogs. Like all amphibians, bullfrogs are cold-blooded. That means the temperature inside their body changes as the outside temperature changes.

Pesticides such as atrazine make frogs more vulnerable to parasites. And pesticides can also cause strange frog deformities. Sometimes those deformities aren't as obvious as missing or shriveled legs. Yet hidden deformities can still harm frogs. That's what Tyrone found when he tested frogs exposed to atrazine.

A Bell's horned frog gulps down a newborn mouse below. It is sometimes called the Pac Man frog after the munching video game creature. Instead of chasing its prey, the Pac Man sits and waits like a web-footed couch potato.

BELL'S HORNED FROG

GLASS FROG

The Amphibian Ark

In June 2005, Ron Gagliardo and Joe Mendelson arrived in Atlanta, Georgia, with a specially modified carry-on suitcase full of frogs. "What else can you do when a whole community is going to be wiped out?" asks Ron, amphibian conservation coordinator at the Atlanta Botanical Garden.

A few months before this amphibian airlift, scientist Karen Lips reported that the deadly chytrid fungus (which had already devastated frog populations in Costa Rica) was moving southeast. It would soon strike frogs living in the El Valle region of Panama. Many of El Valle's frog species live nowhere else in the world. The Panamanian government asked Ron Gagliardo and Joe Mendelson to take some of the rare frogs to the Atlanta Botanical Garden and Zoo Atlanta and breed them in captivity. Several hundred frogs representing more than thirty species were collected, placed in vented plastic deli cups filled with damp moss, and flown to Atlanta.

As the evacuated frogs adjusted to their new home, the Houston Zoo in Houston, Texas,

PANAMANIAN
GOLDEN FROGS

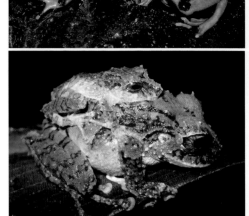

PANAMA ROBBER
FROGS

HORNED
MARSUPIAL
FROG

HOUSTON
TOAD

LEMUR LEAF
FROG

BOB'S ROBBER
FROG

CANAL ZONE
TREE FROG

CASQUE HEADED
TREE FROG

CORONATED
TREE FROG

MUSHROOM
TONGUE
SALAMANDER

stepped in to help the Panamanians build their own captive breeding facility. The building was still under construction in April 2006 when dead frogs turned up in El Valle. In desperation, frog conservationists rented two rooms in a nearby tourist lodge. "The local Hotel Camprestre became our frog hotel," says Paul Crump, a keeper at the Houston Zoo. The guests in rooms 28 and 29 included Panamanian golden frogs, lemur leaf frogs, Bob's robber frogs, and marsupial horned frogs: in total, about three hundred frogs representing thirty species. The effort had come just in time. Within a year the fungus had killed most of the wild frogs remaining in El Valle.

The frogs in Atlanta and those at the new El Valle Amphibian Rescue Center are part of the vision of the Amphibian Ark organization. Amphibian Ark hopes to establish captive breeding programs for five hundred endangered amphibian species. When threats (such as the chytrid fungus) are brought under control, captive-bred animals will be released back into the wild.

LA LOMA
ROBBER FROG

The Amphibian Ark idea isn't limited to exotic Panamanian frogs. The Houston toad, endangered by habitat loss and drought, is getting a boost from a captive breeding program at the Houston Zoo. The zoo released about a thousand juvenile Houston toads into the wild in 2007.

As the Amphibian Ark's motto says: "Frogs matter. Jump in!"

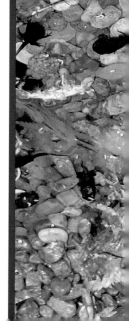

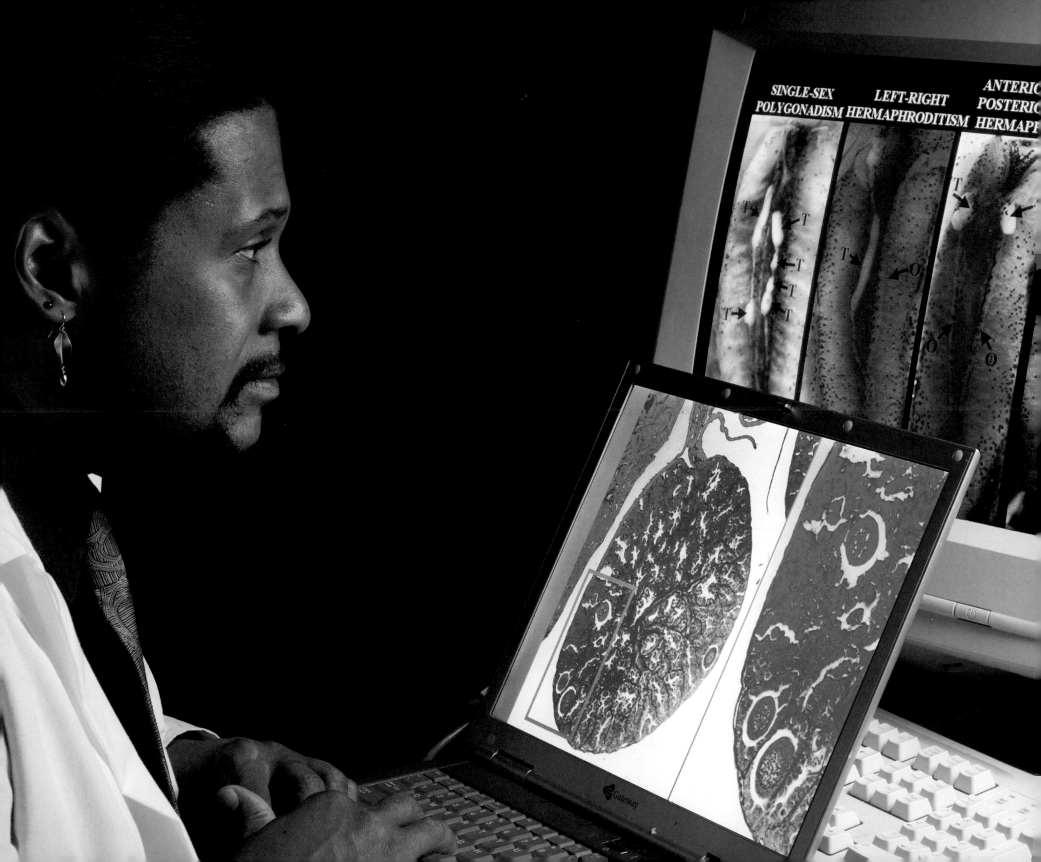

In many frog species the tadpoles are almost transparent.

Gut

Heart

Gills

Follow the Water

Young remembers her first day in Tyrone's lab. Tyrone had just returned from a field trip. Tyrone drove from California to Wyoming with several of his students, spent five hours collecting buckets of water from different study sites, then turned around and drove straight back to Berkeley. "When I saw Tyrone stagger out of the car, his hair was sticking straight up all over, and his eyes were bloodshot," says Young, laughing. "He's a maniac."

Tyrone is known for working hard—especially when there is a lot at stake.

Tyrone often works on two computers at once. The larger computer screen shows deformities in African clawed frogs. The laptop screen shows the testes of a deformed male leopard frog. The circles inside the testes are eggs.

Tyrone realized the pesticide atrazine was a problem a few years ago, when he first tested it on frogs. It is important to know if atrazine is safe because 75 million pounds of the pesticide are put into our environment every year. Atrazine may break down relatively quickly in ponds and streams (over a few months), but it is used heavily each spring. "It is the top-selling product of the world's largest chemical company," says Tyrone. "It's used on corn, the largest crop in the United States. All that atrazine makes its way into surface water and ground water. It ends up in places very far from cornfields."

Companies that make pesticides are required by the U.S. government to test their products for safety. Syngenta, the company that makes atrazine, hired Tyrone to test atrazine on frogs. Tyrone set up a lab experiment with African clawed frogs. Some were raised in clean water and some were raised in water with atrazine in it.

Frogs are ideal for this kind of experiment. They are living sponges, soaking up whatever is in their water. They are also small and easy to care for. "We can test thousands of frogs at once in the lab," says Tyrone.

African clawed frogs are often used for laboratory studies. They may be goofy-looking, but they are hardy and easy to keep in captivity.

1. Every spring, female leopard frogs lay clutches of 600 to 7,600 eggs. Unfortunately, springtime is also when farmers spray pesticides on their crops.

2. Tadpoles eat decaying plants and algae. They don't have teeth, so they rasp algae off rocks and aquatic plants with a small scraper in their mouth.

3. After a few weeks, the developing frog's hind legs emerge.

4. The young frog slowly reabsorbs its tail into its body. By the time its forelimbs appear, its gills have been replaced by lungs. Now the growing frog must come to the surface to breathe.

5. This juvenile frog's tail is almost gone. Once this happens, young frogs hop out into the world. They may journey several miles from the pond where they grew up.

The frogs Tyrone raised in atrazine-contaminated water didn't look different on the outside from the ones raised in clean water. Tyrone dissected (cut apart) dead frogs and looked at their tissues under a microscope. The female African clawed frogs were normal. However, some of the male frogs raised in atrazine-contaminated water had both testes (male reproductive organs) and ovaries (female reproductive organs). They were normal males on the outside, but on the inside they were bizarre half-males, half-females. What was going on?

Tyrone thinks atrazine is an endocrine disruptor. The pesticide confuses the frogs' endocrine system—the system that makes hormones. Hormones are chemicals made naturally by the body. They control the development of a frog from egg to tadpole to adult. Hormones turn chicks into chickens, puppies into dogs, and boys and girls into men and women. "Hormones turn everything on," says Tyrone. "They are like chemical switches."

Atrazine seems to switch on a chemical in the frogs' bodies that turns the male hormone (testosterone) into the female

hormone (estrogen). When atrazine switched on estrogen production in the male frogs, they were feminized.

But perhaps the African clawed frogs were unusually sensitive. Would atrazine have the same effect on a different kind of frog? Tyrone repeated his African clawed frog experiments with leopard frogs. Leopard frogs are found in many parts of the United States. Like African clawed frogs, leopard frogs are often used in laboratory experiments.

Some of the male leopard frogs exposed to atrazine grew eggs instead of sperm in their testes. They were feminized, just like the African clawed frogs. Tyrone found he didn't need a lot of atrazine to feminize male leopard frogs. The atrazine feminized the males at very low levels of contamination—one-tenth of one part per billion.

How small is that? Imagine taking a chunk of atrazine the size of an aspirin. Cut it into ten pieces, and dissolve just one of those teeny pieces into an Olympic-size swimming pool. You'd have about one-tenth of one part per billion of atrazine in the water.

The U.S. government sets health standards for drinking water. The standards say that water with three parts per billion of atrazine is safe to drink. That's *thirty times* more atrazine than Tyrone needed to feminize male frogs.

Syngenta, the company that makes atrazine, refused to let Tyrone publish the

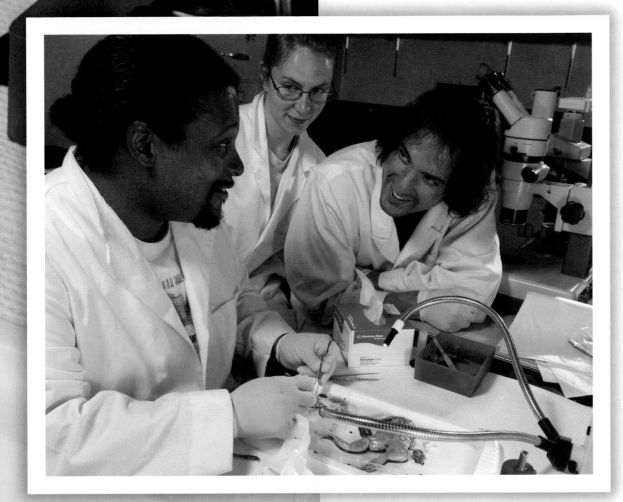

ABOVE
Tyrone shows his graduate students Theresa Stueve and Paul Falso how to find the larynx (voice box) in the throat of an African clawed frog. Some of the male frogs Tyrone exposed to atrazine developed deformed larynges as well as deformed reproductive organs.

LEFT
Tyrone dissects an African clawed frog under a small, powerful light.

results of his research. Publishing articles in science journals is important because that is the way scientists let others know the outcome of their experiments. So Tyrone quit working for Syngenta. He repeated his laboratory experiments, just to be sure. The results were the same.

Tyrone knew, however, that his laboratory experiments were not enough. African clawed frogs and leopard frogs were feminized by atrazine in the lab, but that didn't mean that the same thing would happen *outside* the lab.

That's when Tyrone hit the road.

He rented a big truck and drove from California to the Iowa-Illinois border with some of his Berkeley students. Tyrone and his team visited golf courses, wildlife areas, farms, and wetlands. At every site they collected leopard frog eggs, juvenile leopard frogs, and buckets of water. Tyrone found that about a third of all male leopard frogs in the wild were feminized if they came from places with atrazine in the water. At one site more than 90 percent of the males had eggs in their testes instead of sperm.

"I realized that if male frogs can't reproduce, atrazine might be responsible for some of the decline in frogs and other amphibians," says Tyrone.

However, Tyrone knew that it would take a lot more work to convince other scientists, the government, and the makers of atrazine that the pesticide was harming frogs.

Tyrone's Question

An experiment is a question which Science poses to Nature, and a measurement is the recording of Nature's response.

—Max Planck,
Nobel Prize–winning physicist

It's early on a September morning in Tyrone's frog lab, where heavy metal doors lead to temperature-controlled rooms. Each room has shelves full of white bins, and squirming inside the bins are hundreds of little leopard frogs and tadpoles. They were raised from eggs Tyrone collected at Dugway Pond last April. When the eggs hatched, the tadpoles didn't wiggle out into Wyoming waters. They found themselves in dozens of little plastic ponds in Berkeley, California.

Some juvenile leopard frogs from Wyoming live in Tyrone's laboratory. Tyrone and his students sometimes care for as many as 40,000 frogs and tadpoles.

Date Rec'd Aug 10 2005   Sex juveniles

Source Dugway Pond Wyoming

②

LLS-573

Farah, Young, Jasmin, and Miriam care for tadpoles in Tyrone's laboratory.

Young Kim-Parker, Jasmin Reyes, Farah Syed, and Miriam Olivera have been caring for these tadpoles for months. Although the hours are long, the students don't mind.

"We are here because we want to be here," Young says. "We really care about this work."

The students move quickly. There is a lot to be done. They help each other into lab smocks, pull on gloves, and open the door to one of the rooms. Each student pulls out a treatment set—a group of plastic bins full of tadpoles and juvenile frogs. In each treatment set the frogs are growing up in a different kind of water. Some are raised in clean water and some in water contaminated with atrazine.

Miriam carefully scoops tadpoles out of a bin and into a plastic deli cup. The tadpoles stay in the deli cup while Miriam changes the water.

The net, the deli cup, the bin, and the water jug are all marked with the same colored tapes. Each treatment set has its own special color code. Everything is marked because it is important that no water, tadpoles, or equipment from one treatment set get mixed up with another treatment set. If it did, it would ruin the experiment.

Every scientific experiment begins with a hypothesis. A hypothesis is an idea that the experiment is designed to test. Tyrone's hypothesis is that if frogs are raised in water contaminated by atrazine, then many of the males will be feminized (they will grow eggs in their testes instead of sperm).

To test his hypothesis, Tyrone uses a manipulated variable (something that is deliberately changed, or manipulated) and a responding variable (something measurable that responds to the change). The best way of remembering which is which is to think of an "if . . . then" statement. Tyrone's hypothesis says that **IF** he raises frogs in water contaminated by atrazine (the water is the manipulated variable), **THEN** many males will be feminized (the male frogs are the responding variable).

Scientific experiments need a control group, too. The control group doesn't have the manipulated variable. That means the frogs in one treatment set will grow up in water that doesn't have any atrazine in it. At the end of the experiment the frogs in the control group will be compared to the frogs that *did* grow up in atrazine-contaminated water. If atrazine is feminizing the male frogs, there shouldn't

The different colors of tape on the bins represent different treatment sets. The plastic tubes sticking into the color-coded bins pump air into the tadpoles' water.

be any feminized males in the control group.

Tyrone and his students go to great lengths to make sure everything is identical in the experiment except for the kind of water the tadpoles live in. Young, Jasmin, Farah, and Miriam clean and feed the tadpoles on a strict schedule. All tadpoles get the same type and amount of food. The light levels and temperatures in the rooms are carefully controlled. The students even shift the bins to different positions on their shelf on a regular schedule. That way no bin gets more light or heat than the others. Scientists try to make sure that the only thing that varies in an experiment is the manipulated variable.

This is a blind experiment, too. Young, Jasmin, Farah, and Miriam know that some treatment sets have pure water and some treatment sets have atrazine-contaminated water. But they don't know which is which. Scientists create blind experiments to make sure the people working on the experiment aren't in some small way influencing the results.

Only Tyrone knows what the color codes on the treatment sets mean. Every few days he takes the color-coded jugs and carefully prepares the water. For example, if the black-orange-blue color code is the control group, the water must be atrazine-free. Tyrone will always fill that jug with pure water. If blue-yellow-yellow means

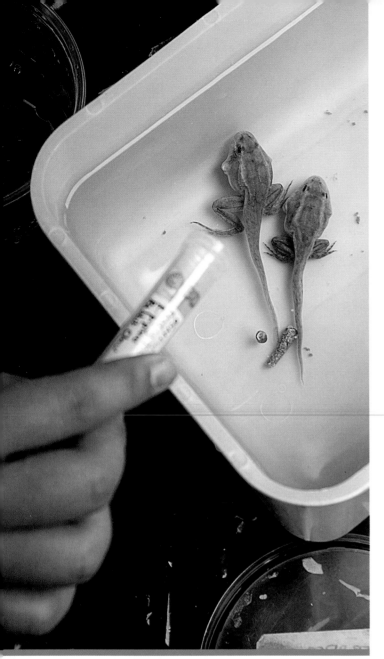

ABOVE
Feeding time at the frog zoo. The tadpoles grow up on a steady diet of rabbit chow.

RIGHT
A juvenile leopard frog raised in the lab.

water contaminated with three parts per billion of atrazine, Tyrone always mixes up water with exactly three parts per billion of atrazine and puts it into the blue-yellow-yellow jug.

Jasmin picks up a deli cup and looks carefully at the tadpoles inside. A tadpole's hind legs emerge first; when the forelegs emerge, the tadpole needs a slightly different bin setup. Jasmin sees that one of the tadpoles in the deli cup is sprouting forelegs. She fishes out the tadpole and puts it in a bin with other foreleg-sprouting tadpoles from that treatment set. This bin has folded paper towels the tadpoles can crawl on, and less water. "We don't feed them in these bins, because once their forelimbs emerge they don't eat," explains Jasmin. "They get nutrients by absorbing their own tail."

Farah checks each tadpole with forelimbs (front legs). Some still have a long, thick tail. Others have only a tiny nub. When the tadpoles have reabsorbed their tail, they have become juvenile frogs. These little frogs are headed to the main lab room. Hopefully, they'll provide some answers about atrazine.

Long hours in the lab create strong friendships. "We are really a family," says Jasmin.

Jasmin, like Tyrone, struggled during her first year of college. She was terribly homesick and flunked a biology class. Then

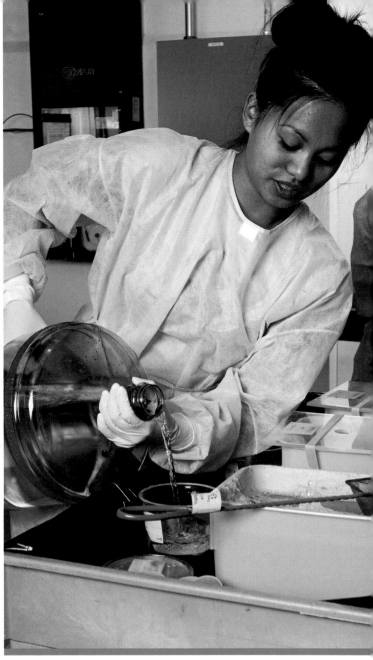

ABOVE
Jasmin puts water in a deli cup for tadpoles while their bin water is changed.

LEFT
Tyrone mixes water for use in his lab experiments.

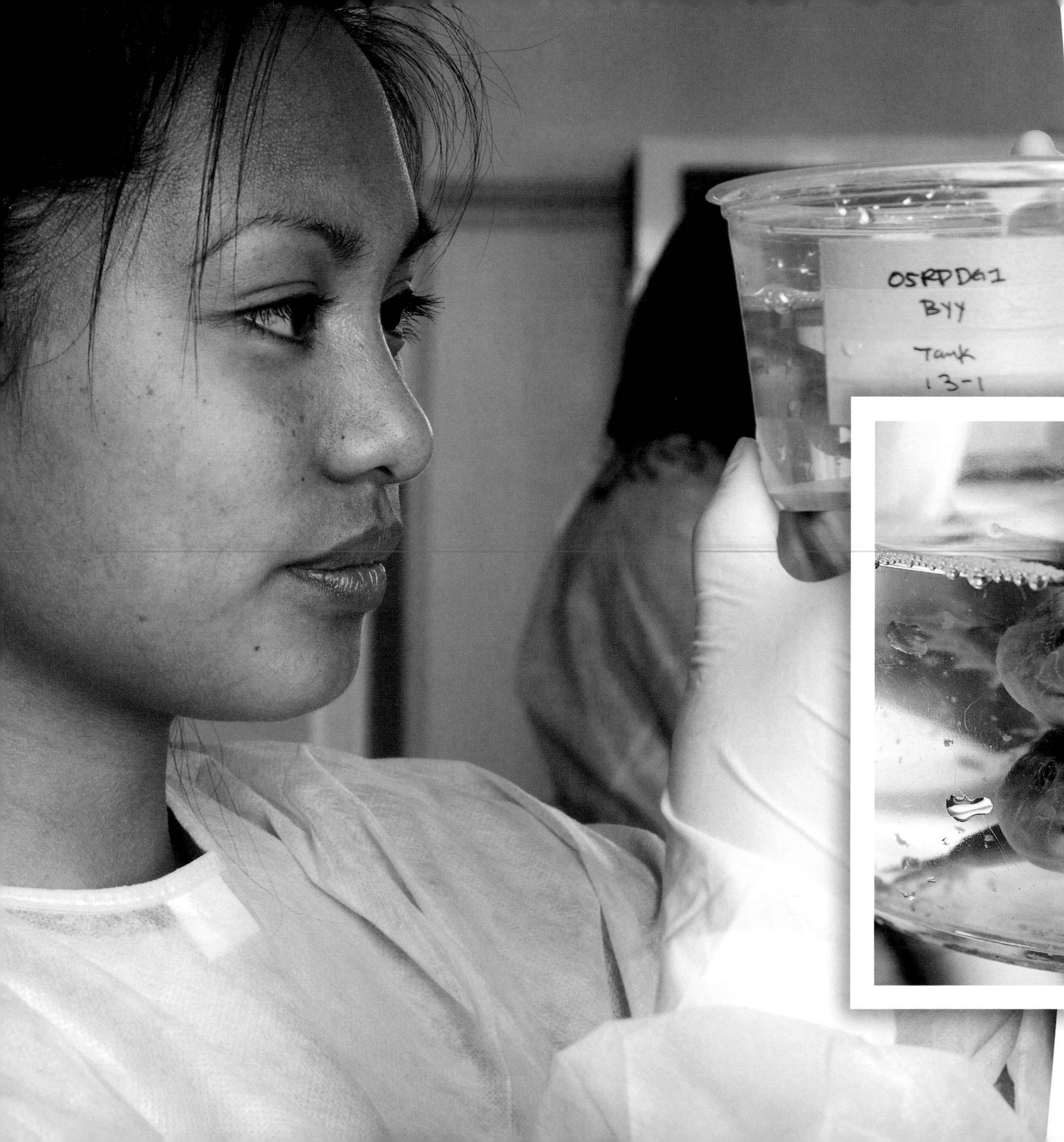

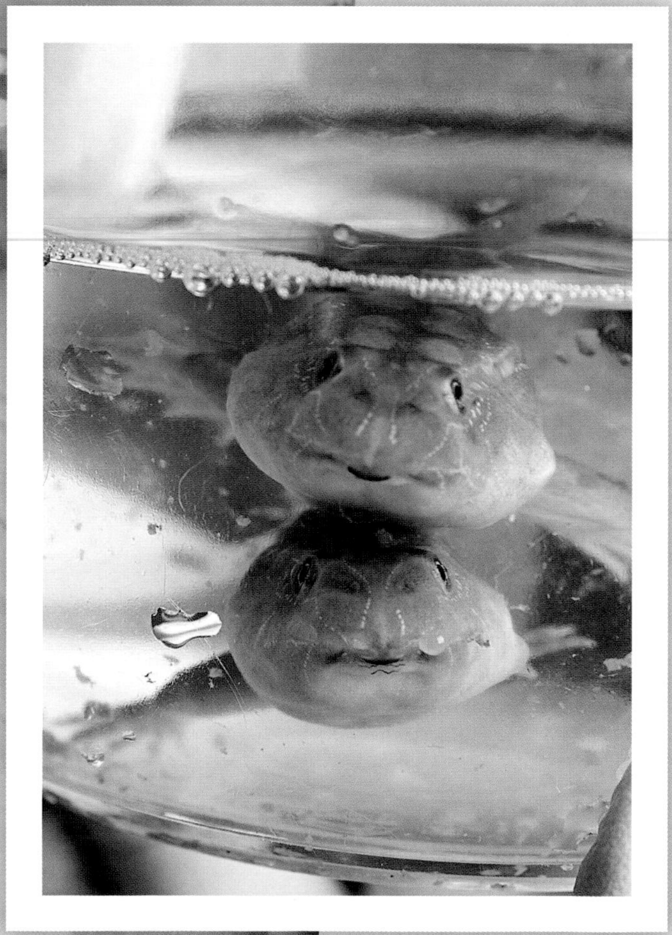

LEFT
Jasmin checks a growing frog.

BELOW
Two leopard frog tadpoles peek out of a deli cup.

Jasmin took a class from Tyrone. He invited her to work in his lab. "This has given me the confidence to do anything," says Jasmin. Now she plans to become a doctor. Young and Farah also hope to go to medical school.

Miriam has a special reason for studying pesticides in Tyrone's lab. She comes from a farming family and spent her weekends and school breaks helping her parents pick strawberries, tomatoes, tomatillos, and zucchini. "If pesticides like atrazine are harmful to people, farm workers are likely to be harmed the most," says Miriam. She plans to work on environmental problems facing farm workers when she graduates from Berkeley.

Tyrone encourages his students to discover what they love and work hard at it. And he has never forgotten his difficult times at Harvard. Everyone in Tyrone's lab gets to do research and go on field trips. Everyone also shares the not-so-fun jobs like washing test tubes. "I look for students who are reliable, persistent, and enthusiastic," Tyrone says. "I would never give up on a student because he or she is struggling in school."

When Young finishes her work in the lab, she goes home to Charlene, her pet green tree frog. She remembers catching tadpoles in a stream when she was little. "I loved all the Frog and Toad books, too," says Young.

Although lame hoppers compared to their frogs, Tyrone and his students do their best at a party in Tyrone's backyard.

Tyrone and his students get together for regular dinner-and-movie nights at his house. There are also special events like the annual Fifth of July barbecue, an all-American celebration with a slight twist. The Fifth of July is a tradition handed down to Tyrone by his father. "I'm not celebrating Independence Day," Romeo Hayes told his son, "because on July Fourth, 1776, our people weren't free."

At the end of every school year Tyrone also throws a Summer Kickoff and Talent Show. Some students have shown their artistic flair by playing the saw and harmonica. Others have performed belly dances, hula dances, Pakistani dances, and Tahitian dances. One student tap-danced—along with his dancing pet ferret!

Tyrone's talent?

"I can open a can of tuna with my teeth," says Tyrone. "That's as good as it gets."

Tyrone's talents do include practical jokes. He once hid a fake plastic finger inside the chili bowl of a very prim student. Another student, who found lobsters very creepy, got a handmade jack-in-the-box as a holiday gift. When she turned the crank, out flew a real lobster shell, complete with wavy legs and antennae!

"You should've heard the screams," says Tyrone with a wicked laugh.

TYRONE'S EXPERIMENT

HYPOTHESIS (what Tyrone thinks will happen): Male leopard frogs that grow up in atrazine-contaminated water will be feminized (their testes will grow eggs instead of sperm). The male leopard frogs that grow up in water without atrazine will develop normally.

Wild leopard frogs lay eggs in Dugway Pond. Tyrone tests the pond water. It is not contaminated with atrazine.

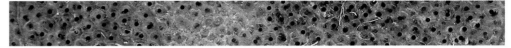

Tyrone collects a few clutches of leopard frog eggs from the pond.

Tyrone puts a small pinch of atrazine in the pond water.

Some frogs grow up in the wild in atrazine-contaminated water. Atrazine is the *manipulated variable*.

Some frogs grow up in the lab in atrazine-contaminated water. Again, atrazine is the *manipulated variable*.

Some frogs grow up in the lab in water without atrazine. This is the *control group*.

Tyrone, Tyler, Young, and Jasmin collect frogs from Dugway Pond.

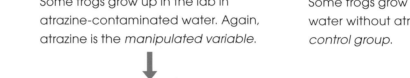

Tissues from all of the male frogs are examined under the microscope. Will some of the male frogs be feminized?

Nature's Answer

Tyrone's main lab room is stacked high with colored tapes, jars of preserved frogs, and hundreds of boxes of slides. The slides hold tiny pieces of frog tissue. The slides will help answer the question: Did atrazine cause deformities in Dugway Pond's male frogs?

One of the froglets from a treatment set is placed in a liquid that will put it permanently to sleep.

Miriam weighs and measures the limp frog
as Farah records the data. Farah gives the
frog a number and notes which treatment
set the frog came from. This same number
will stay with the frog's tissues as they are
analyzed. Eventually, the number will be
matched back to the frog's treatment set.

Next the frog is placed in a chemical
that will preserve its body. Later the frog
will be dissected. If the frog is a male,
its kidneys and testes will be removed.
Unfortunately, there is no way to tell the sex
of a juvenile frog without dissecting it and
looking at its internal organs.

The next step is preparing the male
frog tissue (the kidneys and testes) so the
tissue can be examined under a microscope.
The study of tissue using a microscope is
called histology.

The kidney and testes tissue is put in
special chemicals that will draw out the
water. Then the tissue is bathed in liquid
wax, which hardens into a block. The tiny
bits of frog tissue must be embedded in

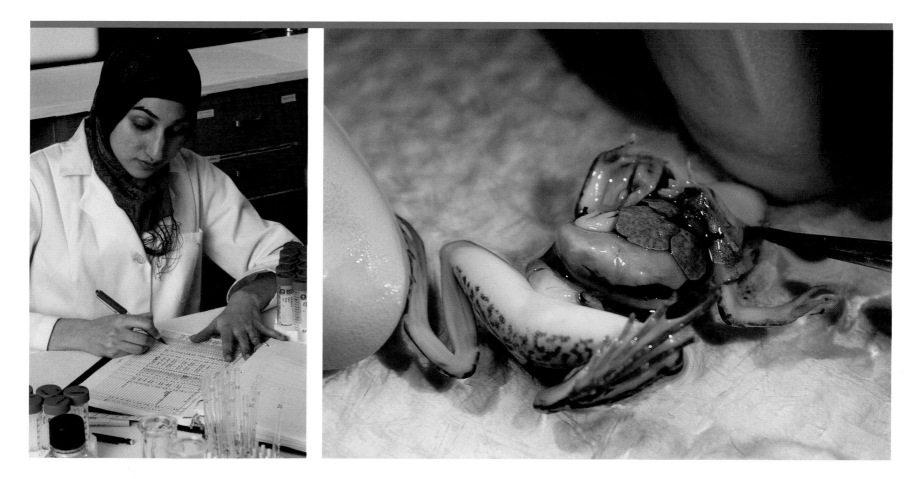

41

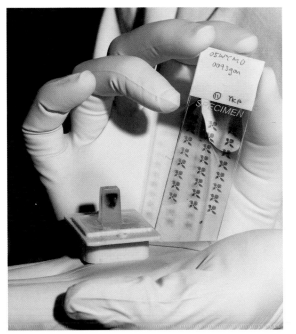

ABOVE
The small white block on the pink square holds a young frog's kidneys and testes. The wax block is sliced into super-thin pieces and stuck to a slide—shown on the right.

RIGHT
Farah puts the wax block into a machine that slices it into a very long, very thin ribbon. Next, the thin slices are stuck onto a glass slide using a special glue.

wax because the tissue must be cut into thin slices for viewing under the microscope. If the frog tissue were still full of water, slicing the tissue would be like trying to cut a wet sponge—it would simply squish down.

Farah puts a wax square holding frog tissue into a special slicing machine. The machine spits out a super-thin ribbon. Farah snips the ribbon into sections and lays the sections on glass slides. Although the frog tissue is no bigger than a grain of rice, it is sliced so thin that a dozen slides are usually needed for all the cross-sections of one frog's kidneys and testes.

As Farah cuts wax blocks, Young and Jasmin dip slides into glass cubes full of colored liquid. The rainbow hues look like something you'd find in an artist's studio, not in a science lab. But the different colors will dye different parts of the frog tissue. Colored tissue is easier to see under the microscope.

Nearby, Tyrone peers through the microscope at a finished slide. Are the testes normal, or deformed? Since this is a blind experiment, Tyrone doesn't know anything about the frog when he looks at its tissue. He doesn't know if this frog grew up in atrazine-contaminated water or pure water. Only much later will the number on the slide be matched to the frog's treatment set.

For this single experiment Tyrone and his students will prepare and examine thousands of slides. Why is all this work

necessary? Why is Tyrone doing more experiments with atrazine, when his first experiments already showed that atrazine can deform frogs?

In science, one experiment isn't the last word on a subject. Many scientists may do similar experiments and get different results. A scientific "truth" is usually decided after *a lot* of argument over data from *a lot* of experiments done *by a lot* of scientists. Each of Tyrone's experiments is a voice in the argument over the safety

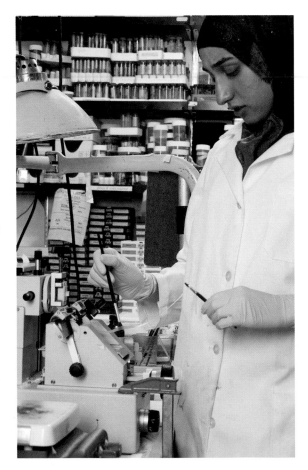

ABOVE
Jasmin, Tyrone, and Young carefully study slides of frog tissue.

LEFT
Glass slides with slices of frog tissue are put in a basket and dunked into a colorful stain. Different stains are used to highlight different kinds of tissue.

43

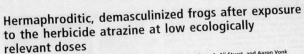

Hermaphroditic, demasculinized frogs after exposure to the herbicide atrazine at low ecologically relevant doses

Tyrone B. Hayes*, Atif Collins, Melissa Lee, Magdelena Mendoza, Nigel Noriega, A. Ali Stuart, and Aaron Vonk

Laboratory for Integrative Studies in Amphibian Biology, Group in Endocrinology, Museum of Vertebrate Zoology, Department of Integrative Biology, University of California, Berkeley, CA 94720-3140

brief communication

Feminization of male frogs in the wild

Water-borne herbicide threatens amphibian populations in parts of the United States.

Atrazine-Induced Hermaphroditism at 0.1 ppb in American Leopard Frogs (Rana pipiens): Laboratory and Field Evidence

Tyrone Hayes, Kelly Haston, Mable Tsui, Anhthu Hoang, Cathryn Haeffele, and Aaron Vonk

Laboratory for Integrative Studies in Amphibian Biology, Group in Endocrinology, Museum of Vertebrate Zoology, and Department of Integrative Biology, University of California, Berkeley, California, USA

THE JOURNAL OF EXPERIMENTAL ZOOLOGY 271:112–119

Factors Influencing Testosterone Metabolism by Anuran Larvae

TYRONE B. HAYES AND PAUL LICHT
Department of Integrative Biology (T.B.H., P.L.) and Department of Molecular and Cellular Biology (T.B.H.), University of California, Berkeley, California 94720

Forum

There Is No Denying This: Defusing the Confusion about Atrazine

TYRONE B. HAYES

Keywords: atrazine, amphibian, endocrine disruptor, chemical castration, feminization

---

When your teacher asks you to write about an experiment in science class, you're learning the basic format all scientists use to report their results. These are a few of the articles Tyrone has written about his frog experiments.

At last, all the slides have been examined, and the numbers on all the slides have been matched back to the treatment sets. The results are in—and they're puzzling.

There were forty male frogs in the control group. All came from eggs taken from Dugway Pond in the spring. All of the frogs in the control group were raised in Tyrone's lab in pure water (no atrazine).

About two hundred male frogs were raised in the lab in atrazine-contaminated water. Like the control group, all came from eggs taken from Dugway Pond.

Tyrone expected that many of the male frogs raised in atrazine-contaminated water would have eggs in their testes instead of sperm. "Instead, we found many cells that look, at least at first glance, very underdeveloped," says Tyrone. "We found underdeveloped cells not only in the male frogs exposed to atrazine, but also in the males from the control group, the group that didn't get any atrazine."

There were twenty males among the juvenile frogs that Tyrone, Young, Jasmin, and Tyler collected at Dugway Pond in August. These males had grown up in the wild, but in water contaminated by atrazine. Eighteen of those twenty frogs, or 90 percent, had eggs instead of sperm in their testes. They were feminized.

Why didn't the cells of frogs exposed to atrazine in the lab look like the cells of frogs exposed to atrazine in the wild? Tyrone thinks the most likely explanation is that in the lab, the frogs were dissected at the very beginning of their juvenile stage (just at the time when the frog's tail is reabsorbed into its body). But although all the wild-caught frogs were juveniles, there was no way to know exactly how old they were when they were caught.

"I think the cells of the lab-raised frogs were less developed because the lab-raised frogs are generally younger than the wild-raised frogs," explains Tyrone.

Tyrone carefully reexamined some of the underdeveloped cells under a microscope. The largest ones turned out to be egg cells. Now all the slides from the lab-raised frogs are being reanalyzed. "We're counting and measuring all those cells that appear underdeveloped," says Tyrone. "We have to figure out which are really egg cells. I think then we'll see a difference between the frogs that were exposed to atrazine and those that were not."

That's the thing about experiments: Even with careful planning, you can't always control everything. And sometimes you have to take a second look.

Why does Tyrone still suspect that atrazine caused the feminized male frogs at Dugway Pond? After all, something other than atrazine might have triggered the growth of eggs instead of sperm in their testes. "Long before I did this experiment, I monitored Dugway," says Tyrone. "Every year I took water samples and collected juvenile frogs. Some years I found atrazine in the water and some years I didn't. But whenever I found atrazine in Dugway Pond, I also found feminized frogs."

Independence, Persistence, Prudence . . . and Balance

W hen Tyrone was in high school he wanted to pierce his ear.

"No son of mine is going to wear an earring as long as he's under my roof," Tyrone's father told him. "But when you leave home, you can do what you want."

As soon as he got to Harvard, Tyrone pierced his ear. "That one represents independence," he says.

Tyrone pierced his other ear when the results of his first atrazine experiments were published in an important scientific journal. Years of hard work went into those experiments. "That one," says Tyrone, "was for persistence."

A few years later his daughter, Kassina, asked to have her ears pierced. Tyrone decided to do it himself. "I botched the job and felt so guilty that I put another piercing in one of my own ears," says Tyrone. "That one represents prudence."

This left Tyrone with two piercings in one ear and only one in the other. So he added a fourth. Explains Tyrone: "Along with independence, persistence, and prudence, you also need balance."

Tyrone will continue to need his independence, persistence, prudence, and sense of balance. He knows the debate over pesticide safety will continue for a long time.

You may be wondering why a pesticide such as atrazine is still being used. In fact, it isn't used everywhere. Atrazine is banned in Europe. However, the United States has (so far) chosen not to ban the chemical. After learning about Tyrone's experiments, the company that makes atrazine hired other scientists to study atrazine's effect on frogs. Some of the scientists found deformities and some didn't. The United States government decided more research is needed. The scientific and political debate over atrazine and other pesticides goes on.

It is often difficult to get a popular pesticide such as atrazine banned. Pesticides are useful because they allow more food to be grown at a lower cost. But cheap food can come with a price tag that isn't on the cereal box or loaf of bread. That price may be ponds without frogs and water we may hesitate to drink.

Tyrone is still seeking answers to the question of how pesticides affect frogs. He has looked at different kinds of amphibians in different kinds of environments. He conducted experiments using spadefoot toads, a species that lives in dry areas of the American Southwest. In the spring they breed in pools of water. As the spadefoot tadpoles grow into frogs, their pools gradually dry up in the heat. Pesticides are left behind as the water evaporates. "But spadefoot toads don't seem to be affected by pesticides," he says.

Tyrone also studied tadpoles in California's Salinas River. Once there were red-legged frogs all over California. The author Mark Twain wrote a famous story about a red-legged frog called "The Celebrated Jumping Frog of Calaveras County." There is still an annual frog-jumping competition in Calaveras County, but the competitors are mostly bullfrogs. Bullfrogs, which are native to the eastern United States, have taken over much of the red-legged frog's habitat. Tyrone saw only one adult red-legged frog during his

WESTERN SPADEFOOT
TOAD

ABOVE

One-Eye is one of Tyrone's favorite toads. When Tyrone found her in the central valley of California several years ago, she was already missing an eye—probably a wound left by a predator. One-Eye is the mother of most of the little spadefoots in the toad spa, says Tyrone: "She's one tough mama."

LEFT

Tyrone visits the toad spa, an outdoor pen where he raises western spadefoot toads.

CALIFORNIA RED-LEGGED FROG

study of the Salinas River, so he focused on bullfrogs instead.

Tyrone found that bullfrog tadpoles living in the upper part of the Salinas River, where the water comes from a clean reservoir, were growing up strong and healthy. However, the tadpoles growing up downstream were much smaller. That part of the Salinas River is contaminated by a mix of pesticides from nearby farms.

Tyrone began to wonder: how do mixes of pesticides affect frogs? Most scientists look at one pesticide at a time. Yet frogs living in the wild, such as the bullfrog tadpoles, often live in a pesticide stew. So Tyrone and his students researched nine different pesticides, including atrazine. They found that if tadpoles were raised in water with just one pesticide, almost all of them survived. But if tadpoles were raised in water with a mix of all nine pesticides, a third died.

"Maybe out in the real world, atrazine alone isn't the most important thing," says Tyrone. "Maybe we should also be looking at the big picture—how mixes of pesticides, including atrazine, affect frogs."

How much of amphibian decline is caused by pesticides? "I think many different things are responsible, like habitat loss, global warming, and disease," says Tyrone. "But I do think pesticides have a major impact on wild amphibians

ABOVE
The U.S. Environmental Protection Agency temporarily banned sixty-six pesticides from parts of California to help protect the red-legged frog.

LEFT
Tyrone is looking at how mixes of pesticides affect frogs. This leopard frog developed in water containing several pesticides. Its body could not fight off an infection that damaged its nervous system. It can no longer hold its head up. Wild frogs affected this way would quickly be eaten be predators.

and are contributing to amphibian declines."

All this has made Tyrone aware that research isn't enough. He has given more than three hundred talks to scientists, government officials, farm workers, and young people. "If I can't teach people about my research," he says, "then the impact of my research is limited."

At Prospect Sierra School in El Cerrito, California, Tyrone talks to his son Tyler's class about the amazing transformation frogs undergo: "From an egg to a creature with gills, then to a living, breathing system just like you."

Tyrone explains his research and how male frogs can become feminized by atrazine. "If that's in the water we are drinking, why don't we turn into females, too?" a boy asks.

Tyrone explains that humans aren't like frogs. We don't grow up in the water. We don't breathe through our skin. Human males aren't feminized by pesticides like male frogs. Yet we're still connected to our environment, just like the frogs.

What if these pesticides cause human health problems? Tyrone points out that farm workers—many of them low-income people with poor access to doctors—face the highest risk. "Guys who spread atrazine on cornfields have the stuff in their urine at levels 24,000 higher than the level that

makes male frogs grow eggs," Tyrone says. "If one of these guys peed in a bucket, there would be enough atrazine in his urine to feminize thousands of frogs."

In the end, paying attention to the health of our environment isn't just something for frog scientists, farm workers, or government officials. It's for everyone. As Tyrone says: "Environmental health and human health are one and the same."

ABOVE
The bullfrog tadpole on the left grew up in a part of the Salinas River that is polluted by pesticides. The bullfrog tadpole on the right grew up in a clean part of the river.

Glossary

AMPHIBIAN: a member of the scientific group of animals that includes frogs, toads, salamanders, and caecilians (legless amphibians that look like worms and live in the tropics).

ATRAZINE: a man-made chemical designed to kill weeds.

BLIND EXPERIMENT: a technique used to prevent bias in an experiment. In a blind experiment, color codes or numbers are used to prevent the researcher from knowing which group is receiving which treatment.

CAECILIAN: an amphibian that looks like a worm and lives in the tropics.

CHYTRID FUNGUS: a fungal disease scientists believe is responsible for the decline of many amphibian populations around the world.

CONTROL GROUP: a group used as a standard of comparison in an experiment. A control group is as similar to the experimental group as possible but doesn't receive the treatment under investigation.

EGGS: the reproductive cells produced by females.

ENDOCRINE DISRUPTOR: a chemical that interferes with the normal functioning of the endocrine system.

ENDOCRINE SYSTEM: a system of glands that regulates the body and produces hormones.

ESTROGEN: a hormone that regulates the development of sex characteristics in females.

EXPERIMENT: the testing of a hypothesis under controlled conditions.

HISTOLOGY: a branch of biology involving the study of plant and animal tissues using a microscope.

HORMONE: a chemical made by the body's endocrine system that controls growth and development.

HYPOTHESIS: a tentative explanation or working idea that can be tested.

INTRODUCED SPECIES: a species that is not native to an ecosystem.

KIDNEYS: a pair of bean-shaped organs that filter wastes from the blood and excrete the wastes (mixed with water) as urine.

MANIPULATED VARIABLE: the factor the experimenter decides to change, or manipulate, in an experiment. Everything else in the experiment is kept the same.

OZONE: a special form of oxygen. Ozone in the earth's atmosphere helps block damaging ultraviolet radiation from the sun.

PESTICIDE: a man-made chemical designed to kill pests such as weeds or insects.

RESPONDING VARIABLE: the factor the experimenter measures to see if the manipulated variable had any effect.

SPERM: the reproductive cells produced by males.

TESTES: the male reproductive organ that produces sperm.

TESTOSTERONE: a hormone that regulates the development of sex characteristics in males.

THEORY: a well-tested, widely accepted explanation for a group of facts, observations, and data.

Featured Frogs and Toads

AFRICAN CLAWED FROG
Xenopus laevis
Southern Africa

AMERICAN BULLFROG
Rana catesbeiana
Eastern and Midwestern
United States

**AMERICAN GREEN
TREE FROG**
Hyla cinerea
Southeastern United States

BELL'S HORNED FROG
Ceratophrys ornata
South America

BLUE POISON DART FROG
Dendrobates azureus
South America

**BUMBLEBEE POISON
DART FROG**
Dendrobates leucomelas
South America

**CALIFORNIA
RED-LEGGED FROG**
Rana draytonii
Western United States
(California)

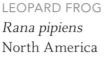

LEOPARD FROG
Rana pipiens
North America

**MOUNTAIN
YELLOW-LEGGED FROG**
Rana muscosa
Western United States
(California)

PAMPAS TOAD
Melanophryniscus stelzneri
South America

RED-BANDED RUBBER FROG
Phrynomantis bifasciatus
Sub-Saharan Africa

RED-EYED TREE FROG
Agalychinis callidryas
Central America, Columbia

RED-LEGGED WALKING FROG
Kassina maculate
Eastern Africa

ROCOCO TOAD
Bufo schneideri
South America

SONORAN DESERT TOAD
Bufo alvarius
Western United States

SONORAN GREEN TOAD
Bufo retiformis
Western United States

**STRAWBERRY POISON DART
FROG**
Oophaga pumilio
Central America

WAXY-MONKEY TREE FROG
Phyllomedusa sauvagii
South America

WESTERN SPADEFOOT TOAD
Spea hammondii
California, Northern Mexico

WHITE'S TREE FROG
Litoria caerulea
Australasia

A Note on Frogs vs. Toads

What is the difference between a frog
and a toad? Most people think of
frogs as having moist, smooth skin and
long hind legs, while toads have drier,
bumpier skin and shorter hind legs.

The scientific definition is different.
Scientists classify all true toads in the
family and genus *Bufo*. The Sonoran
green toad, Sonoran desert toad, and
rococo toad are true toads. The western
spadefoot toad, despite its common
name, is actually a frog.

Helping Frogs in Your Community

— Organize a cleanup of local ponds and streams.
— Make sure your garden products are nontoxic.
— Find out what kind of frogs live near you and learn more about them.
— Teach others about frogs and the problems they face.

Websites

Tyrone maintains his own website, with the ironic address www.atrazinelovers.com. At the bottom of the "About Tyrone Hayes" page are links to many articles about Tyrone and the controversy over atrazine.

National Geographic named Tyrone one of their "Emerging Explorers." Find out more at www.nationalgeographic.com/emerging/tyroneHayes.html.

San Francisco's Exploratorium has a special website full of frog facts: www.exploratorium.edu/frogs. Plus, there's a page just on Tyrone: www.exploratorium.edu/frogs/researcher/index.html.

Frogwatch USA uses volunteers around the country to help scientists monitor frog populations. Kids welcome! www.nwf.org/frogwatchUSA

A Thousand Friends of Frogs, a project of the Center for Global Environmental Education at Hamline University, began when middle school students in Minnesota discovered malformed frogs. Its website is designed especially for children. cgee.hamline.edu/frogs/students/index.html

The Declining Amphibians Task Force has the latest on amphibian decline and amphibian research. www.open.ac.uk/daptf/index.htm

AmphibiaWeb maintains a searchable database on the world's amphibians. amphibiaweb.org

The Amphibian Ark is the center of an effort to establish breeding populations of highly endangered amphibians in zoos around the world. www.amphibianark.org

Of Special Interest to Educators

National Geographic has developed a series of K–12 lesson plans on Tyrone's work. See the "Lesson Plans" link at the bottom of the "Emerging Explorer" page at www.nationalgeographic.com/emerging/tyroneHayes.html.

Multimedia

Strange Days on Planet Earth ("Troubled Waters" episode). National Geographic Society, Washington, D.C., 2005. A segment of the episode is devoted to Tyrone and his students; parts were filmed at Dugway Pond.

Selected Scientific Bibliography

Hayes, Tyrone B. "There Is No Denying This: Defusing the Confusion About Atrazine." *BioScience* 54, no. 12 (Dec. 2004): 1138–49.

——. "Welcome to the Revolution: Integrative Biology and Assessing the Impact of Endocrine Disruptors on Environmental and Public Health." *Integrative and Comparative Biology* 45, no. 2 (April 2005): 321–29.

Hayes, Tyrone B., Atif Collins, Melissa Lee, Magdelena Mendora, et al. "Hermaphroditic, Demasculinized Frogs After Exposure to the Herbicide Atrazine at Low Ecologically Relevant Doses." *Proceedings of the National Academy of Sciences* 99, no. 8 (April 16, 2002): 5476–80.

Hayes, Tyrone B., Kelly Haston, Mable Tsui, Anhthu Hoang, et al. "Atrazine-Induced Hermaphroditism at 0.1 ppb in American Leopard Frogs (*Rana pipiens*): Laboratory and Field Evidence." *Environmental Health Perspectives* 111, no. 4 (April 2003): 568–75.

——. "Feminization of Male Frogs in the Wild." *Nature* 419 (Oct. 31, 2002): 895–96.

Lannoo, Michael, ed. *Amphibian Declines: The Conservation and Status of United States Species.* Berkeley: University of California Press, 2005.

Stuart, S. N., J. S. Chanson, N. A. Cox, B. E. Young, et al. "Status and Trends of Amphibian Declines and Extinctions World-wide." *Science* 306, no. 5702 (Dec. 3, 2004): 1783–86.

A Note on the Experiment

Tyrone Hayes's experiment using frog eggs and juvenile frogs from Dugway Pond had additional levels of complexity not detailed in this text. Frogs in the treatment sets in Tyrone's laboratory were exposed to five different concentrations of atrazine (from .01 to 10 parts per billion). The entire experiment was also conducted under a cool temperature (18 degrees Celsius), a warm temperature (28 degrees Celsius), and a progressive temperature (rising gradually from 18 to 26 degrees Celsius).

Acknowledgments

First and foremost, we would like to thank Tyrone Hayes for his willingness to include us in everything from field trips to laboratory work to impromptu dinners at his home. It was fascinating, of course, but above all, it was fun. We owe a special thanks to Tyrone's wife, Kathy Kim, and his children, Tyler and Kassina.

The assistance, enthusiasm, and good humor of the Hayes Lab students: Sina Akhavan, Travis Brown, Paul Falso, Anna Fellman, Vicky Khoury, Laura Meehan, Anne Narayan, Mary Stice, Theresa Stueve, and especially Young Kim-Parker, Sherrie Gallipeau, Miriam Olivera, Jasmin Reyes, and Farah Syed, was much appreciated. You make us want to go back to college.

The author is indebted to Tyrone Hayes, Connor Townsend, Carol Peterson, Nancy Humphrey Case, Keely Parrack, and Deborah Underwood for their critique of this manuscript. Many thanks to Ron Gagliardo of the Atlanta Botanical Garden and Paul Crump of the Houston Zoo for sharing their experiences with the Amphibian Ark project; Mr. Crump also provided rare frog images. The photographer would like to thank Andrew and Raquel Charek, Darby Cunningham, Robert E. Espinoza, and Brian Weber for allowing him to photograph various frog species, and Alice Abela, Chris Conroy, and Sara L. Schuster, who contributed hard-to-get images. Our editor at Houghton Mifflin, Erica Zappy, was a valuable friend and advocate all along the way. We greatly appreciate her guidance and encouragement. To YAY! Design we owe a debt for the stunning book design.

Last, thanks to all the frogs who posed so patiently. The next round of crickets is on us.

Index Page numbers in *italics* refer to illustrations.

Photo credits:

Pages 1–4: Pamela S. Turner

5, top (great blue heron):
Getty Images

6–7: Pamela S. Turner

9–11: Hayes family archives

14, lower right (golden toad):
Museum of Vertebrate Zoology,
UC Berkeley

16, left (deformed leopard frog):
A. B. Sheldon

20–21: Paul Crump

25, top left (embryos):
James H. Harding

37, top (embryos): Nathan
Nazdrowicz; left (Tyrone at
Dugway Pond): Pamela S. Turner

50, top (red-legged frog): Alice
Abela; bottom (leopard frog):
Dr. Tyrone Hayes

51 (tadpoles): Laura Oda

All other photographs by Andy Comins

AMERICAN GREEN TREE FROG